TALKING WITH CHILDREN AND YOUNG PEOPLE ABOUT DEATH AND DYING

SECOND EDITION

Mary Turner

Illustrated by Bob Thomas

Jessica Kingsley Publishers
London and Philadelphia

DEDICATED TO THE MEMORY OF BOB THOMAS

First edition published in 1998
This edition published in 2006
by Jessica Kingsley Publishers
116 Pentonville Road
London N1 9JB, UK
and
400 Market Street, Suite 400
Philadelphia, PA 19106, USA

www.jkp.com

Library of Congress Cataloging in Publication Data

Turner, Mary, 1933-
    Talking with children and young people about death and dying / Mary Turner ; illustrated by Bob Thomas. — 2nd ed.
        p. cm.
    Includes bibliographical references.
    ISBN-13: 978-1-84310-441-4 (alk. paper)
    ISBN-10: 1-84310-441-5 (alk. paper)
    1. Children and death. 2. Bereavement in children. 3. Grief in children. I. Thomas, Bob. II. Title.

    BF723.D3T87 2007
    155.9'37083—dc22

                                                                2006025681
British Library Cataloguing in Publication Data

ISBN-13: 978 1 84310 441 4
ISBN-10: 1 84310 441 5

Printed and bound in Great Britain by
Printwise (Haverhill) Ltd, Suffolk

Contents

Please note before reading

This resource is designed for adults to read selectively with children and young people. Do not give it in its entirety to a young person to read alone. Adults should read Part One thoroughly before proceeding.

Any page of this book may be photocopied for use in therapy or as an overhead projection. Multiple copies may not be taken nor may copies be taken for use in material to be sold.

PART ONE

FOR THE HELPER

**Please read this thoroughly
before proceeding**

Introduction

This resource is designed to help adults (be they family, friends, professional helpers, or others) to communicate with children and young people on the subjects of death and dying, and to help them to express their thoughts and feelings, fears and questions. This resource is suitable to be adapted for use with children and young people of any age, and can be modified to meet individual needs according to beliefs and cultural backgrounds.

Please read the *whole* of Part One of this book before proceeding to use the material in Part Two, which is designed for direct use with children and young people.

I have discovered the need for this resource book through my work with grieving young people and their families. Most of the youngsters I have met have expressed profound and often frightening thoughts, fears and worries when encouraged to open up. These may manifest themselves in dreams, day dreams, physical problems, or behaviour. They often stem from a great sense of loss and insecurity, perhaps as a result of the serious illness or death of someone close. We cannot usually put right the loss, but we can gently help a young person to express something of the inner turmoil they are experiencing; and we can help to answer questions, clarify misunderstandings, and calm many irrational fears. It is surprising how quickly a child will feel a little better, or his/her family will notice an improvement in behavioural problems, once an opportunity has been provided to spend time with someone calm and reliable who can give time and space for this work to be done. It would seem that if a fear, rational or otherwise, can be somehow acknowledged, or 'given a name', then some healing can begin to take place. A fear or worry that is well received by someone else can be diminished in the sharing.

Somehow, published material in the form of the written word can assume a particular weight of authority. I have found this useful to bear in mind when attempting to reassure children and young people who often keep their worries private in the lonely belief that their situation, thoughts or beliefs are quite unique and intransigent. Powerful misconceptions have been eradicated from a grieving child's life by showing him/her appropriate pages from Part Two.

This material is intended to help address factual issues such as what happens to us when we die, and also to address issues relating to what might be going on inside a child's mind as he/she tries to handle what is happening and his/her reactions to events. The pain of bereavement for a child or young person is often compounded by the nature of the relationship had with the person who has died, the circumstances of the death, and by practical worries about the present and the future. An opportunity is provided to air these concerns. It is recognised that many fears can be exacerbated by television programmes, films and computer games: material is included to enable expression of problems arising from this. The needs of the young person both at home and at school are taken into account.

It is not always easy to meet with a child in their place of suffering. However, it is well documented by experts in the field of childhood grief that strong and empathic adult assistance to a grief-stricken child has very significant immediate positive results, and may well prevent serious mental health problems later on. As we talk about things that distress us, so we are able to process these thoughts and memories, loosening their impact on our minds and bodies.

Grief and extreme distress can manifest themselves in many ways. If we cannot recognise that a child or young person needs help, all the words in the world will be useless. Distress can build up over time due to a combination of events. For example, someone close to a child may be ill for a long time, causing strain on family functioning, stress in relationships, shortage of time to meet pressures from school and peers, and burden of extra tasks – let alone all the worry involved.

Or distress can suddenly assume enormous proportions at a moment's notice, for example when there is an unexpected death.

We need to bear in mind that emotional experiences that are overwhelming for a child – that are too much for him or her to be able to bear – may in fact be experienced as trauma. Trauma can get stuck inside our minds and bodies and can sometimes need additional help in shifting.

> Children may be exposed to a variety of upsetting events that do not (necessarily) meet the official criteria for trauma, such as death of a family member, family breakup, serious illness, and geographical displacement… Children's symptoms following such things are often suggestive of a post traumatic reaction. For children at least, there may be relatively little difference between an unexpected traumatic experience and an unavoidable major loss experience that has been expected: the overwhelming fear and helplessness may be present in either case… Our concern should be not how bad the trauma is according to some objective criterion, but rather how it is affecting the child now. (Greenwald, 2001, p.276)

In the next section, 'Manifestations of Distress in Children and Young People', you will find some guidelines on what you might expect a child to be experiencing, and how it might affect them both in mind and body.

Also included in Part One is a brief summary of ten practical points for bereaved adults. Since a core message in this resource is the need for adults and children to remain connected, it seems appropriate to offer some guidance to bereaved adults who may be caring for bereaved children and young people.

Those of us trying to help grieving children need to make ourselves available to tune into the reality of the child's experience, whilst remaining grounded and supported in what we do. It is very important to take care of ourselves, and to obtain help or supervision, especially if we are feeling somehow out of our depth.

The organisations listed under Useful References and Contacts p.22–24 provide you with both up-to-date details of helpful resources, and local contacts for any additional help that you might require.

This resource book is prepared with love to all the children and their families who have taught and continue to teach me. It is dedicated to the memory of Bob Thomas, who drew the pictures.

Manifestations of Distress in Children and Young People

There follows below a ten-point summary of what to watch out for in children and young people that may convey, often in non-verbal ways, that they are needing help. Bear in mind that if these behaviours/symptoms do not show signs of resolving over time, the child may be needing more help than you can give. They are all common signs that a child or young person is overloaded with distress that has not been processed. All of the manifestations of distress listed below are very likely to be resolved with patience and understanding; however, they may also be more intransigent signs of trauma. The material in Part Two will help you address these manifestations.

We need to be aware of how a young person might be communicating without words. Whatever age we are, we do not always express to other people what we are feeling and thinking after something very sad or distressing has happened. There are lots of understandable reasons for this. For a child or young person there can be even more reasons. Children do not always understand what has happened and therefore confusion can be an additional factor. Children do not always have the vocabulary to express themselves, and are therefore left with more non-verbal ways to react to events. Children and young people may be concerned not to draw attention to their own needs for fear of overburdening their adult caregivers even more. It is often very hard for them to know how to talk about their feelings, and how to respond appropriately to each other – these experiences are more likely to be new ones for them and beyond their usual experience. It can therefore be seen that although all the following signs can be present in distressed people of any age, they are very likely to manifest themselves in children and young people.

Remember that a child or young person may have had stress in their lives before their most recent acquaintance with death and bereavement. It is possible that manifestations of distress that were present before could therefore be exacerbated.

Reliving/re-experiencing a distressing event

The child may play or behave in ways that somehow recreate or relive elements of the difficult event. He or she may be preoccupied with the event and ask worried questions, constantly think about it, show it in drawings, or act it out. The child may experience intrusive memories of the event, or be very upset by triggers that remind him or her of the event such as a smell, sight or sound. The child may have sleep disturbances including nightmares, night terrors, sleep walking, and fear of going to sleep. The child may be hypervigilant and always on the alert to danger to him/herself or others.

Avoidance/fear/withdrawal

The child may close down and do everything possible to avoid reminders of the difficult event. He/she may avoid activities and interactions previously enjoyed. New fears may surface, such as those of water, darkness, or people.

Confusion and concentration/memory problems

The child or young person may be very confused about aspects of what has happened, and the implications for him/her. He/she may be very confused about life and death issues. There may be trouble concentrating and doing work, and trouble in remembering what has been said. There may be daydreaming, and difficulty remembering old skills.

Regressive behaviour

Children may regress both in their developmental skills already acquired, and in their behaviour. There may be delays in learning new skills and language according to the normal developmental milestones.

Aggressive behaviour

Watch out for aggressive, defiant and unreasonable behaviour in a child where this has not always been present.

Magical thinking

This is a form of thinking coming from the part of our brain related to the fight/flight response. It is a primitive form of thought that little children often experience in which they perceive themselves as the centre of the world and therefore the cause of everything that happens around them. Children and young people may feel ashamed and guilty that something they did or did not do caused the person to die or to be ill. They may also experience themselves as having new omnipotent powers such as the ability to foresee omens.

Separation difficulties

Children and young people may show problems in being separated from people they depend upon and feel secure with. They may exhibit crying and clinginess when expected to leave someone they feel safe with. They may not want to go to school or playgroup or college. They may be constantly worried about the where-abouts and the safety of people who care for them.

Changes of relationship with parents/carers/peers

Children and young people may show a profound change in how they relate to people around them. Where relationships were secure they may now become difficult. The child may be critical of, or worried about, how others are reacting to what has happened. This can lead to alienation from people the child previously had a close relationship with. Children can be concerned about showing their distress and may therefore try to mask it. This can be particularly true of teenagers who need to feel that they are the same as all their peers. Adults so often want to believe that children are managing in their grief that they often contribute to this alienation by overlooking the child's distress.

Physical symptoms (somatisation)

Stress can upset the balance of the body leading to any number of genuine physical problems. A child may also manifest strange symptoms that do not seem to point to a particular medical diagnosis: such problems may also be caused by unresolved distress.

Sense of foreshortened future

Children and young people may not think that they themselves are going to live for very long, or have meaningful lives.

Try to be mindful of the child you are helping, and to use this list as a guide to help you understand. The organisations listed on p.22–24 can provide you with extra advice and information if required.

Ten Practical Points for Bereaved Adults

1. When we are bereaved we need support. Shock and grief affect people of all ages in many different ways. Try not to let pain and distress separate people from one another.

2. People usually want to help. Let them – providing they do not take everything out of your hands. It is important to feel in control. Now is not the time to feel guilty or feeble about accepting or requesting help: it simply makes sense so that you and the children can get through the days and weeks to come as best you can. Children and young people will feel easier if they know that you are being helped both practically and emotionally by other adults. It is enormously important for children to see that you are not having to manage all by yourself: if they can worry just a little less about you, their overall worries will be lessened.

3. Tell other people, for example teachers at school, what the situation is. Do make sure that the children's playgroup, school, or college know about their bereavement. It can be very helpful to talk to a teacher that you know and trust. The school will then be able to keep an eye on how the children are, and be mindful that if their performance or behaviour changes, there are reasons which may account for these changes.

4. Talk to the children before liaising with other people about them. They may want to know what you are planning to say, or they may have some ideas of their own about what they would like said, and to whom.

5. Make a list or drawing of all the people who love and support the children, or who are their friends. Pin it up where the children will see it and be able to get reassurance from looking at it. Tell the children that these people will help and care for them. It is nice to draw all these people in a circle with the children in the middle. Try to show the drawing to some of these people. The children may want to do this themselves, or they may want someone to help them.

6. The above example is just one way of helping to promote a child's resilience, or ability to cope, in the face of adversity: 'Resilience is a universal capacity which allows a person, group or community to prevent, mimimise or overcome the damaging effects of adversity' (Grotberg 1995, p.7). Anything you can think of to boost a child's self esteem at this time will be extremely important and will help him or her feel a little stronger inside. Remind a child or young person of all the things they have achieved or coped with in their lives; encourage and praise them as much as possible. Provide opportunities for them to succeed in new things.

7. Help the mind and body to stay as steady as possible, and to be as free of stress as possible – whatever age you are. Remember that what we eat and drink is important. Drinking plenty of pure water helps the system to function. Nutritional supplements can support the body in times of stress. You may like to consider herbal and homoeopathic remedies that are especially to be recommended for young children and babies for whom medication is not usually advised. Acupuncture can be very useful but is not generally used with younger children. Massage can be very soothing and should be considered for little babies and upwards. Try lavender oil sprinkled in bath water or onto a pillow. Do not put it directly onto the skin. It is calming and helps with sleep.

8. Consult your doctor if symptoms of distress do not begin to ease. Remember that more specialised help is available for us when we are depressed or traumatised – and it does not always need medication. You may also find the contacts listed on p.22–24 of use to you.

9. Be patient with yourself and with the children as time goes by. Try to look after yourself and to find a little time away from sad things. It is important for everyone to know that somehow life can go on and that it is OK to enjoy yourself.

10. Try not to feel guilty if some happiness finds its way into your life. The people who have put this book together hope it does, and wish you well.

How to Use This Resource

This resource is designed to be used with individual children and young people, or with groups, in a supportive setting only. **It is not designed for a child to read alone.**

- These pages are yours to use in whatever way and in whatever combination you wish: mix and match them to suit the needs of the young person you are working with (and to suit your own needs too!). Select appropriate pages according to the individual situation of each child. For example, separate pages are provided on the different ways in which we manage the disposal of the body after death.

- Photocopy pages as you wish.

- Add pages with your own, or the child's material, as you wish. You might wish to create your own special book.

- Remember to include, if necessary, additional material as appropriate for each child's cultural and religious background. These pages are a base to proceed from.

- Decide with the young person who will take care of any material that is created as a result of using this resource. You may choose to keep some pages and destroy others. Children may appreciate your taking charge of any difficult material. Treat the material respectfully. It may need a cover.

- Don't give the young person these introductory pages. Begin with Part Two, from 'This belongs to…' The subjects for facilitated discussion are listed on the contents page at the front of this book (p.3).

- Be careful not to work automatically through every page without regard to the young person's needs. It is not helpful to overload with unsought-after information. Perhaps talking about death and dying can be compared to talking about the 'facts of life'; be sensitive to how you impart information, and mindful as to whether it is of help.

- Once you have read through all these pages, which you are advised to do before you begin in order to give you an overview of what you might expect to crop up, you may decide you can go ahead without directly using any of them. Fine! If this resource helps to tool you for the task ahead, it has achieved its purpose.

- Complement and supplement this work with other creative work with the young person, for example preparing a memory box, painting, modelling, dancing, and reminiscing.

- Don't be afraid to be creative. Children respond well to imaginative adults.

- Be informed. Read around on the subject. The references provided here are not only useful guidelines for this work with children, but also contain many useful suggestions for books to read with children.

Do not proceed without reading the next section, 'Things to Consider Before You Begin'.

Things to Consider Before You Begin

- What networks are in place for the young person apart from yourself? Have you discussed this with those who are caring for the child? Does the system include parents, relatives, teachers and others? How can you link together in support of the child and his/her family?

- Who is the most appropriate person to talk to the child? Is it that the family need help to handle these issues themselves, or do they wish for extra help?

- Do you plan to have someone else with you and the child; might it be helpful to have another family member present, for example?

- What are the specific belief systems for this family? Do you need to liaise with anyone about this?

- What arrangements will you make about confidentiality?

- Your agreement with the young person. Can you keep to it?

- Children may well act out their distress. Grief can be manifested by us all in many ways other than talking about it. Behaviour can be affected when a child finds an adult who gives permission to get in touch with the pain. Is the support system ready for this? **Go gently.**

- How will you end? Plan carefully.

- How do you look after yourself?

- **It is very unwise to do this work without supervision. Refer on, or consult, when in doubt.**

Useful References and Contacts

Many of the references provided below contain further suggestions for useful reading, and for material for direct use with children and young people. The contacts listed below will be able to provide relevant and contemporary details of available resources and materials.

Useful references

Barnard, P., Morland, M. and Nagy, J. (1999) *Children, Bereavement and Trauma: Nurturing Resilience.* London: Jessica Kingsley Publishers.

Christ, G.H. (2000) *Healing Children's Grief: Surviving a Parent's Death From Cancer.* New York: OUP.

Crossley, D. (2000) *Muddles Puddles and Sunshine: Your Activity Book When Someone Has Died.* Stroud: Hawthorne Press.

Crossley, D. and Stokes, J. (2001) *Beyond the Rough Rock: Supporting a Child Who Has Been Bereaved Through Suicide.* Cheltenham: Winston's Wish.

Goldman, L. (2006) *Children Also Grieve: Talking about Death and Healing.* London: Jessica Kingsley Publishers.

Granot, T. (2004) *Without You: Children and Young People Growing Up with Loss and its Effects.* London: Jessica Kingsley Publishers.

Greenwald, R. (1999) *Eye Movement Desensitisation Reprocessing (EMDR) in Child and Adolescent Psychotherapy.* New Jersey: Jason Aronson.

Grotberg, E. (1995) *A Guide to Promoting Resilience in Children.* The Hague: Bernard van Leer Foundation.

Holland, J., Dance, R., MacManus, N. and Stitt, C. (2005) *Lost for Words: Loss and Bereavement Awareness Training.* London: Jessica Kingsley Publishers.

Holland, J. (2001) *Understanding Children's Experiences of Parental Bereavement.* London: Jessica Kingsley Publishers.

Jones, E.H. (2001) *Bibliotherapy for Bereaved Children: Healing Reading.* London: Jessica Kingsley Publishers.

Mallon, B. (1998) *Helping Children to Manage Loss: Positive Strategies for Renewal and Growth.* London: Jessica Kingsley Publishers.

Mood, P. and Whittaker, L. (2001) *Finding a Way Through When Someone Close has Died: What it Feels Like and What You Can Do to Help Yourself: A Workbook by Young People for Young People.* London: Jessica Kingsley Publishers.

Munroe, B. and Kraus, F. (eds) (2005) *Brief Intervention with Bereaved Children.* Oxford: OUP.

Pearson, M. (1998) *Emotional Healing and Self Esteem: Inner-Life Skills of Relaxation, Visualisation and Meditation for Children and Adolescents.* London: Jessica Kingsley Publishers.

Riches, R. and Dawson, P. (2000) *An Intimate Loneliness: Supporting Bereaved Parents and Siblings.* Maidenhead: Open University Press.

Servan Schreiber, D. (2004) *Healing Without Freud or Prozac.* New York: Rodale.

Silverman, P.R. (2000) *Never Too Young to Know: Death in Children's Lives.* New York: OUP.

Smith, S. (1999) *The Forgotten Mourners: Guidelines for Working With Bereaved Children.* 2nd edition. London: Jessica Kingsley Publishers.

Stokes J. (2000) *The Secret C: Straight Talking About Cancer.* Cheltenham: Winston's Wish.

Stokes J. (2004) *Then, Now and Always. Supporting Children as They Journey Through Grief: A Guide for Practitioners.* Cheltenham: Winston's Wish.

Stokes, J. and Crossley, D. (2001) *As Big as it Gets: Supporting a Child When Someone in the Family is Seriously Ill.* Cheltenham: Winston's Wish.

Turner, M. (2005) *Someone Very Important Has Just Died: Immediate Help for People Caring for Children of All Ages at the Time of a Close Bereavement.* London: Jessica Kingsley Publishers.

Tuzeo-Jarolmen, J. (2007) *When a Family Pet Dies: A Guide to Dealing with Children's Loss.* London: Jessica Kingsley Publishers.

Yalom, I. (1980) 'The Concept of Death in Children.' In I. Yalom (ed) *Existential Psychotherapy.* New York: Basic Books.

Useful contacts in the UK

The Childhood Bereavement Network (CBN)
8 Wakley Street
London EC1V 4ET
Tel: 0207 843 6309
Email: cbn@ncb.org.uk

The CBN will provide you with the name of an organisation or an individual near you who can help you with issues relating to grief and bereavement in children and teenagers.

The Child Bereavement Trust (CBT)
Aston House
High Street
West Wycombe
Bucks HP14 3AG
Tel: 01494 446 648
Website: www.childbereavement.org.uk

The CBT can provide books and information and also has a website forum for bereaved families.

Hospice Information

Hospice House
34–44 Britannia Street
London WC1X 9JG
Tel: 0870 903 3903
Website: www.hospiceinformation.info

Staff at your local hospice may be able to put you in touch with appropriate people in your community who can help.

The British Association for Counselling and Psychotherapy (BACP)

1 Regent Place
Rugby
Warwickshire CV21 2PJ
Tel: 0870 443 5218
Website: www.bacp.co.uk

Cruse Bereavement Care

Cruse House
126 Sheen Road
Richmond
Surrey TW9 1UR
Tel: 0208 939 9530
Website: www.crusebereavementcare.org.uk

Cruse is a national bereavement support service provided by trained volunteers.

Survivors of Bereavement by Suicide (SOBS)

Centre 88
Saner Street
Hull HU3 2TR
Tel: 0870 241 3337
Website: www.uk-sobs.org.uk

SOBS is a national support service run by survivors, for survivors.

The EMDR UK and Ireland Association

www.emdr-uki.org

EMDR International

www.emdria.org

The above are two of the many websites that can provide details of Eye Movement Desensitisation and Reprocessing treatment for trauma-related problems in people of all ages. EMDR is one of the National Institute of Clinical Excellence recommended treatments for trauma. For a good explanation of this treatment, refer to Dr Servan Schreiber's book as listed in the above section.

Useful contacts in the US

The Crisis Center Foundation
Baton Rouge Crisis Intervention Center
4837 Revere Avenue
Baton Rouge, LA 70808
Tel: (225) 924 1431
Website: www.brcic.org

They offer crisis prevention, intervention and postvention services, and have 24-hour availability.

American Association of Suicidology
5221 Wisconsin Avenue, NW
Washington, DC 20015
Tel: (202) 237 2280
Website: www. suicidology.org

Dedicated to the understanding and prevention of suicide.

American Hospice Foundation
2120 L Street, Suite 200
Washington, DC 20037
Tel: (202) 223 0204
Website: www.americanhospice.org

Supporting the needs of dying and grieving Americans.

The Tragedy Assistance Program for Survivors, Inc. (TAPS)
National Headquarters
1621 Connecticut Avenue, NW, Suite 300
Washington, DC 20009
Tel: (202) 588 8277
Hotline: (800) 959 8277
Website: www.taps.org

A support network for those who have died in service to America.

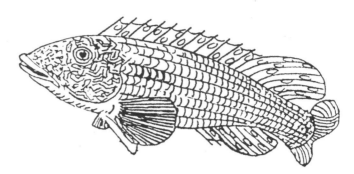

PART TWO

RESOURCE

Subjects for facilitated discussion

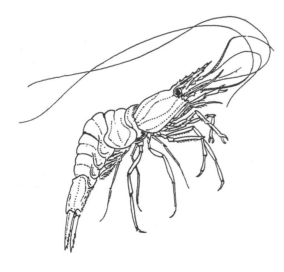

This belongs to...

Introduction

Talking about dying, and about death,
can be very hard.

We may have lots of questions
– and sometimes fears and worries too.

It can be difficult to know whether to try to talk
about how we are feeling and what we are thinking,
or whether it would be better to keep everything
inside us, and not talk to anyone.

This was written for you by Mary, and the pictures were drawn for you by Bob.

Mary has met a lot of very sad children and young people and knows something about the thoughts and feelings, fears and worries you might have.

She has also had some children herself.

These pages should be of help to you in learning about sadness or worries.

We can feel a little less lonely or worried when we have talked about these things, or drawn about them.

Talking, and drawing or writing can help because then our sadness and our worries are not so stuck inside us.

Sometimes we have questions that can be answered once we have asked them.

Perhaps the person who reads these pages with you is a good person to talk to?

Or they can help you think of someone else who you could be with as you look at these pages?

Sometimes we need to be alone. But sometimes it can be good to share with someone else the things we are thinking, feeling, and even dreaming about.

You can use the writing in this book to help you to ask questions and talk about your worries. You can use the pictures to help you too. Colour them in if you like, or add some of your own.

Sometimes it helps to draw a question, or a worry, or a nightmare.

Some of the pages may give you ideas about what you want to talk about, and some may just be good to colour in.

Below, there is a space for you to draw a picture of someone who you like to share your worries with. It can be a person or an animal.

Dying and Death

Living and dying are part of the world we are in.

Living and dying are part of nature,
and we are part of nature.

The world is a wonderful place.
It is marvellous when babies are born.
And it is wonderful when fresh leaves appear
on the trees, or beautiful new flowers bloom.

Sometimes we are sad when summer ends
and the leaves fall from the trees.

It is very sad when people and animals die.

Everything is a part of nature.

These things are part of nature:

trees

birds

rain

sun

Can **you** think of more?

33

Leaves die in the autumn.

Often, before they gently drift from the trees, they turn to many lovely colours.

As they fall they twist and twirl in the wind.

The leaves are flying on the wind, and floating in the air.

They dance together as they land on the ground below.

Have you noticed how very beautiful
leaves are in the autumn?

Have you noticed their special dance as
they float and flutter from
the trees?

The leaves float down from the trees
on to the earth below.

After a while they become part of the earth itself.

Dead leaves are very good for the earth.

They make it a lovely place for the little seeds
to grow in when spring comes.

Little plants and seeds need the earth to grow in.

So dying and growing, death and life, go together.

Have you ever been in a wood,

and seen

and smelled

and touched

the rich beautiful earth beneath the trees?

Think in your own mind of your own special wood.

Your own lovely wood. It may be a real place you
know, or a place you are making in your mind.

Can you write, or draw
what your special wood is like?

My own special wood

Draw it here.

So, each falling leaf is a tiny part of helping
next year's trees and grass and flowers to grow.

Death and life go together.

We are all part of this.

Sometimes when the leaves fall from the trees
we burn them on bonfires.

The ash that is left after the leaves have burned
is very good for the earth.

Everything that lives will die one day:

    dogs and cats

    bees and butterflies

    mums and dads.

Everything that is alive.

How does this make you feel?

'There is a time for every living thing
to grow and flourish and then to die.'

Ecclesiastes 3.1, *The Bible*

'As leaves are, so are the generations of mankind. As for the leaves, some the wind scatters on the ground, and others the budding forest puts forth when spring comes again.

So it is with mankind,
one flourishes and another fades.'
Homer, *Iliad 6*

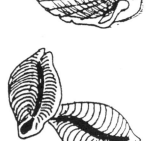

Death happens when a body is too old,
or ill, or damaged, to go on working.

Dying is when the special power of life
leaves the body.

A dead person cannot come back
to life on earth again.

He or she will not need a body any more.

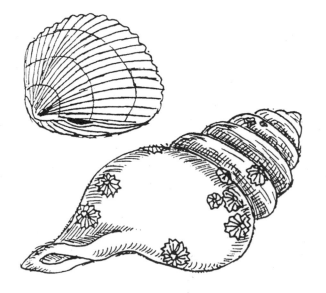

Every day has a beautiful sunrise, and
a beautiful sunset too.

The sun goes down over the horizon,
and it's hard to understand where it
has gone. It slips away from us,
and out of sight.

There are beginnings and endings
all around us.

That is the way things are.

That is the way the world is.

We cannot see where a rainbow ends.

The Bible tells us that God made the rainbows
– and everything else.

He made the world, and when people die
they somehow go back to Him.

He made us, and somehow
we go back to Him.

'Praise be to Allah,
Who created the heavens
And the earth,
And made the darkness
And the light.'
The Koran, 6.1

In the Koran it says that:

'Every soul shall have a taste of death' (21, 35).

It is very sad.

We will all have times when we are very sad
because someone we know,
or a special pet,
has died.

When we are so sad we can feel very lonely.

Nearly everyone is sad sometimes because
someone special, or a special pet, has died.

Or we are sad because we have lost
something very precious.

When we are so sad we can feel very lonely.

What happens when people or animals die?

What do **you** think?

51

When people and animals
die they stop breathing
and they stop thinking.

Their hearts stop beating
and they do not feel
anything.

When things die,
the special part we call 'life',
or 'soul', leaves the body.

It does not ever come
back to the body.

Not ever.

The body is very quiet
and peaceful and still.

For ever.

After a person has died, their body is put in the earth.

The body isn't needed any more.

There is no pain,
and no feelings.

So it is quite all right
for the body to be quiet
and peaceful like this.

The person no longer
lives in the body after
it has died.

Some people call the
special power of life the
'soul' or the 'spirit'.

We do not know exactly what happens to this,
because it cannot come back
to us as a human to tell us.

It is good to feel in our hearts, and know inside ourselves, that something lovely happens to the special part of the person that leaves the body when the body has died.

Perhaps it is something wonderful in the same way that caterpillars turn into butterflies, or eggs turn into little birds that can fly!

Some people are worried or afraid
about what happens to a person
after they have died.

Are you worried about this too?

Would you like to ask a question,
or draw what you are thinking?

Do you have your own idea about what
happens to the special part of a person
after they have died?

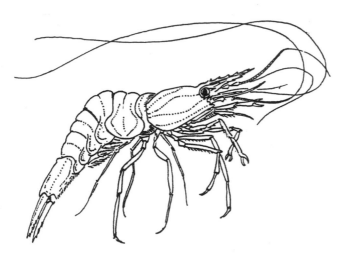

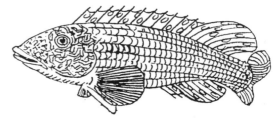

A dead person cannot come back to
life again.

Death is not like sleep.

Dying is not like sleeping.

Sleeping is part of living.

Sleeping helps us to grow, and to feel
stronger when we wake up each day.

It is very sad, but sometimes people
are killed (die) in accidents.

Sometimes bodies are damaged too much
to get better, however hard
the doctors and nurses try to help.

When that happens we are often angry and sad.

Do you know anyone who has died in an accident?

Sometimes people get
very ill and die.

Everyone tries very
hard to help them
to get better.

But sometimes,
however hard
everyone tries, we
cannot stop someone
from dying.

It is very sad.

It can also make us feel very angry,
and lots of other things too.

Do you know anyone
who has been very ill and died?

Sometimes an illness can be inside a person's mind.

This sort of illness may make them not want to go on living any more.

Doctors and other kinds of people, and families too, try very hard to help.

But sometimes the illness cannot be made to go away and then the person feels it would be better to be dead and peaceful.

Then a person might decide to kill themselves, and this is called suicide.

We often feel that it is our fault if someone
commits suicide, but
IT NEVER IS.

Suicide happens when someone is ill
inside their mind in a special sort of way,
and then they decide that no one can help
them.

Sometimes we worry that the
person committed suicide because of us.

If you are thinking this it would be
a good idea to talk about it.

Saying Goodbye, and Thinking About Funerals

After someone has died, their friends and family often come together for a special meeting.

This meeting is called a funeral.

Sometimes the dead body is there to touch or to look at if anyone wants to.

At the funeral the people say goodbye to the body that is not needed any more.

And they think about the special power of life that has left the body.

At a funeral we also talk about the person who has died, and remember how special he or she was.

It is often very sad, but we need to share these things together.

Talking together about the dead person can help us feel a little less lonely inside.

Have you been to a funeral, or been asked if you want to go?

It is OK to talk about this, and ask questions.

Do you have any questions you want to ask right now?

Before the funeral the dead
body is put inside a coffin.

A coffin is a special wooden box.

The coffin has a lid.

Remember:
a dead body doesn't feel
anything, or think anything.

After someone has died we can
sometimes go to see the dead body
in the coffin
so that we can say goodbye to it.

Have you been to see the dead body
of your Special Person who died?

Would you like to talk about that?

Sometimes we do not go to see the dead body to say goodbye.

There are lots of other ways that we can say goodbye later on.

Sometimes we put things inside the
coffin with the dead body.

Some people like to leave special things
with the dead body.

This can be part of our saying goodbye.

Do you know anyone
who has done this?

Sometimes the funeral is in a church.

Have you been to a church funeral?

Would you like to talk about it,
or to ask any questions?

Remember what happens to the leaves?

At the end of the funeral, the dead body is taken
in the coffin to be buried.

The name for the very deep hole which the coffin
is put into is a grave.

The coffin is lowered gently
into the grave.

Later on the grave will be
filled in again with earth.

Have you seen a coffin being put in the ground (buried)?

What was this like?

The coffin is usually buried near a church
(in the churchyard), or in another special
place where bodies are buried.

The name for the place where bodies are
buried is a graveyard, or cemetery.

The coffin is put in the grave, and later on it is covered with earth.

The grave is usually about two metres deep.

Sometimes we put flowers on top of the grave, and later the dead person's family often puts a special stone over the grave, called a headstone.

The headstone is put at the end of the grave. It usually has loving words carved on it that have been chosen by the family of the person who has died. Sometimes the dead person's date of birth and date of death are written on the headstone too.

Have you been to a
graveyard
or cemetery?

What was it like?

Remember the leaves?

Sometimes the dead body is cremated.
This means that the body is taken in the coffin
to a special place called a crematorium.

At the crematorium people meet together
to say goodbye to the dead body.
Then the body is burned (cremated)
in a special very hot oven, and turned into ash.

We do not watch this.

Remember:
the dead body does not think
or feel anymore.

After a dead body has been cremated, the
ashes are put in a very special pot.
Later the ashes can be put somewhere
special.
Lots of people like to scatter ashes
on the ground in a special place.

Remember the leaves?

We are all part of nature.

Do you have any questions?

Have you been to a
crematorium funeral?

Is there anything you would
like to say about it?

Or maybe you have some
questions you would
like to ask?

(There are a lot of questions
on this page, aren't there?!)

Usually people gather
together to say goodbye
to the dead body of the
person who has died,
and to remember
the person.

Sometimes people meet
together in a house,
and sometimes in a
special place
like a mosque.

Have you been to a
special meeting to say
goodbye to a person
who has died?

Sometimes children want to go to the funeral
and sometimes they don't.

What about you?

Do you need to talk to someone about this?

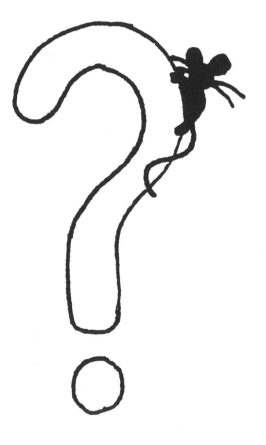

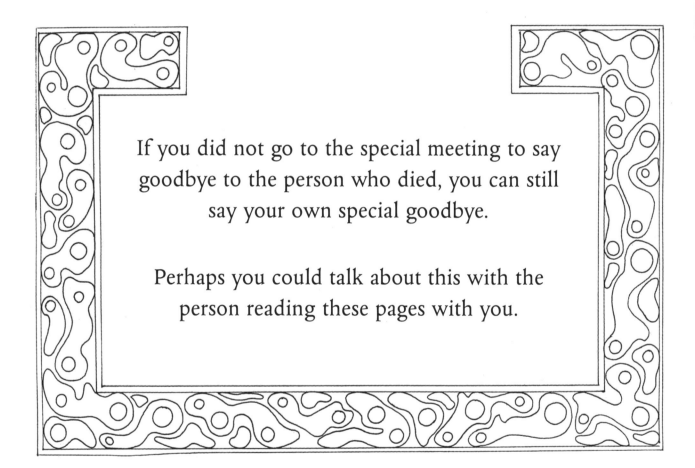

If you did not go to the special meeting to say goodbye to the person who died, you can still say your own special goodbye.

Perhaps you could talk about this with the person reading these pages with you.

Talking About Someone Who Has Died

This is Candy.

Candy was Mary's
special friend.

Candy has died.

Mary still thinks
about Candy, and
talks about her
a lot.

This drawing is
from a photograph
of her.

Mary has the
photo on her wall
at home.

Do you know of a pet that has died?

Or do you know anyone who has died?

What is his or her name?

You can draw a picture below if you like.

Sometimes we know people who are very ill,
or who have had bad accidents.

Do you know of anyone?

What is his or her name?

It can be very sad
talking about dying.
Some children and young people
are scared too.

But it is horrid to keep your feelings
stuck inside you.

Grown-up adults often
find this hard too.

This is a difficult time
for everyone.

Sometimes we have worrying feelings,

or thoughts

or questions

or nightmares.

They stay inside us and we don't know
whether to talk about them or not.

We can feel a little better when we let out some of the things we are thinking or feeling.

It can help to talk a little, or to draw.

Or you can talk and draw a lot if you want to!!!

We will not forget someone special
when they die.

They were too important.

And we need to remember,
even though sometimes it is very hard.

Do you think the person looking at
this with you could help you to talk
about what happened?

Would it help you to remember
your Special Person?

Or maybe you can think of someone
else who could help you in this way?

Or maybe you can talk to a favourite pet?

Mary used to talk to a favourite tree!!!

It is sometimes hard to talk about death and dying.

It can be a big help to talk about things,
but only if you want to.

Shall we stop, or carry on?

Have you any questions so far?

When shall we carry on?

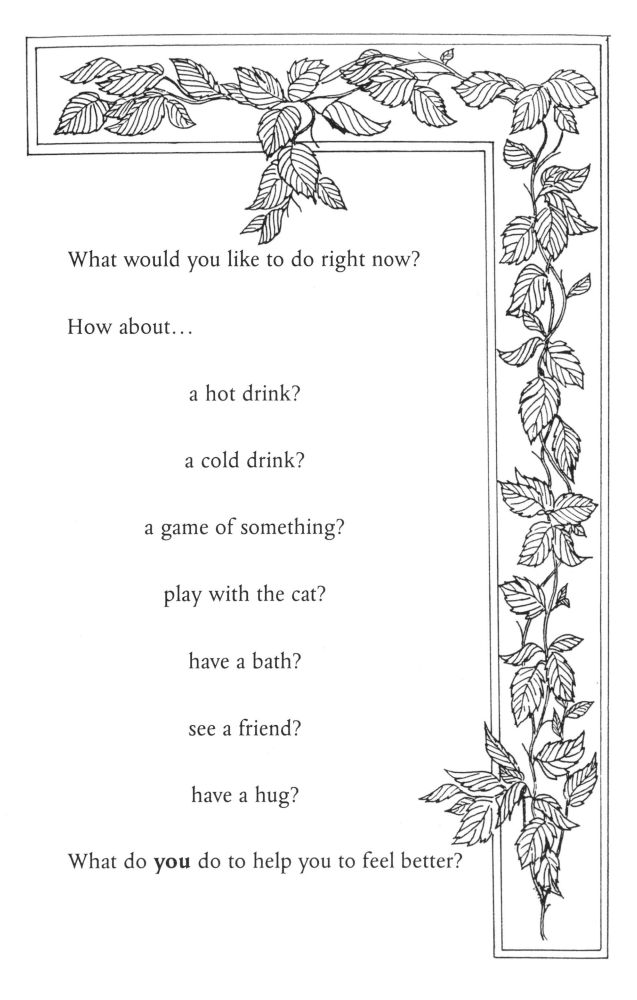

What would you like to do right now?

How about…

a hot drink?

a cold drink?

a game of something?

play with the cat?

have a bath?

see a friend?

have a hug?

What do **you** do to help you to feel better?

Thoughts and Feelings

When someone dies, we feel lots of things and we think lots of things.

Here are some of them:

We may feel that we will never laugh again.
Or we may feel guilty because we have been laughing!
Do any of these things describe you?
Are there some more words to describe what you are thinking and feeling?

I am feeling...

Write down some of your feelings (or would you rather draw?).
Do you know where in your body you have feelings?
Can you draw that?

I am thinking...

Write down some of your thoughts (or would you rather draw?).

Crying can be a good thing to do.

It helps us to let our feelings out.

This is the same for us all,
children and grown-ups,
boys and girls,
men and women.

So do not worry too much if you know
a grown-up who is crying.

He or she will be OK,
and so will you.

Talking and crying together may help
us all to feel less lonely.

We may feel very angry when
someone dies and we
are left the way
we are.
Feeling angry doesn't
make us bad people.

What can we do about being so
angry?

Sometimes, we get worried that even just feeling angry could hurt
someone – but it can't.
Often we find it difficult to tell people that we are angry.
People don't talk about anger much.

But talking (or even drawing) can help to make the anger less strong
inside you.

Here is a list of things that can help when we feel angry…maybe you
have your own ideas too?

Go for a swim.
Go somewhere private and…SHOUT!!!!!!!
Kick a ball.
Talk to a friend.
Talk to the cat (or dog, or…).

My anger

Draw an angry picture.

Sometimes we may feel relieved, or even happy, that the person who has died cannot feel pain anymore.

It is OK to feel like that.

We may even feel glad that someone has died if they had been unkind to us in some way.

This can be very hard to talk about and your mouth feels zipped shut.

Has this happened to you?

If you know someone who is very ill, or someone
who has died, you have probably felt lots of
sad and worrying things.

But you must try to remember that they wouldn't
want you to be sad all the time.

A lady called Joyce Grenfell, who was a famous
comedienne, wrote a (serious) poem before she died,
for the people she would leave behind.
In it she said…

'Cry if you must, but laugh as well.'

It is OK to enjoy yourself
and have fun and good times.

It is more than OK – it is important.

Something that makes me laugh or smile is…

Remember!!!

- Whatever you are feeling, you are not bad…you are sad.

- Your thoughts and feelings cannot make anyone else ill, or hurt anyone.

- Your thoughts and feelings will get easier.

- Be kind to yourself!!!

- Don't blame yourself.

- Don't get cross with yourself.

Fears and Worries

You cannot harm anyone else by talking
about these things, however silly
or bad
or frightening they are to you.

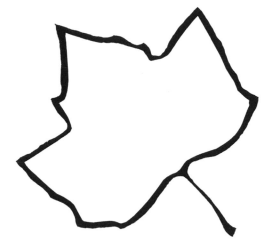

It's OK!

Lots of people feel guilty (cross with themselves) when a loved person dies.

Like somehow it was their fault that the
person died, or they should have done
something different to stop it happening.

We cannot say, or think, anything to make
someone die: although we watch things like
that on TV sometimes.

Maybe you don't feel guilty. You don't need to.

But if you do, it helps to tell someone.

Perhaps you were naughty or bad tempered.

Perhaps you wish that you had done
something, or said something,
or thought something different.

But remember!!!

NOTHING SAID,
                        OR THOUGHT,
COULD MAKE SOMEONE DIE.

Is this a worry for you?

We can sometimes worry
that the person who has
died might be watching us
to make sure we are
behaving ourselves.

This is not true.

When people have died we
think about them, but they
are not watching us to
check-up on us.

Do you have any worries
like this one?

Sometimes we are afraid that we might be very ill, and die too.

Even things like coughs and colds and cuts can be a worry.

Or we might worry that someone else close to us might die.

It is OK to talk about this to someone who will be able to reassure you and answer your questions.

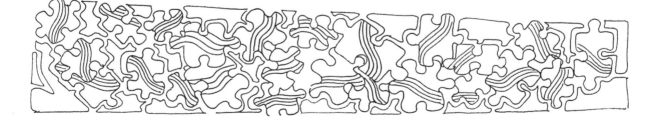

111

Sometimes there are programmes on the TV that worry us.

Or we might see a film or a video about death that is frightening.

Are there any TV programmes
that have bothered you?

or films?

or videos?

It is OK to talk about this…it will help.

The things we watch,
or the things we hear people say,
or even tales other people tell at school,
can sit inside our minds and give us all
sorts of worries.

Has that happened to you?

A lot of the things we are afraid of in our
minds might be only ideas we have got from
films, or books, or TV, or computer games.

These things are not real.

They have been made up by people.

Have you got any worries about these things?

How about drawing, or writing,
or talking about this?

Do you think that might help?

Perhaps someone can help you sort this out a bit?

You may have a big worry – and this is a
BIG one – that whatever you are thinking
can actually happen just because you think it.

So you worry that if you think sad or
horrible things they will really happen
because you think them...

THIS IS NOT TRUE...

But lots of children and young people
have these thoughts. They just don't
talk about them much.

Does this happen to you?

The person reading these pages can
help you.

Talking about something, or thinking about
something, cannot make it happen.

Talking about this worry can help it to go away.

Sometimes we have a fear or
a worry that seems so
horrid, or so peculiar (odd!),
that we don't like to tell
anyone.

This happens to lots of people.

Could you try to talk about this worry?

Or maybe draw it?

We can have a very secret fear or worry that we don't like to talk about.

You will probably feel a lot better if you can talk about it, or draw it.

My worst fear or worry is...

Draw or write it here.

Dreams and Nightmares

We all have good dreams,
and we all have bad dreams (nightmares).

Dreams can seem very real, and sometimes
we think about them a lot after we have
woken up.

Do you ever remember your dreams?

People often dream about someone
who has died.

Do you?

Would you like to talk about these dreams,
or draw them?

Are your dreams good dreams,
or nightmares,
or both?

You cannot make a dream worse by talking about it.

Often bad dreams get less bad when we talk about them…or even draw them.

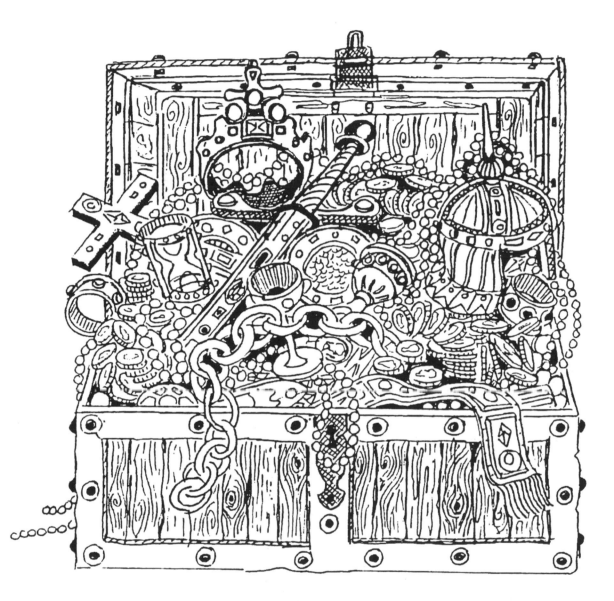

My bad dream

Write or draw it here.

My good dream

Write it or draw it here.

Don't forget that sleep is good for us.

When we close our eyes and go to sleep it is
a time when our bodies grow, and get strong,
and stop being tired.

Sleeping gives us energy.

Do you like going to bed?

Or do you have worries about
going to bed, or being asleep?

Sometimes when it is dark we get scared
because things look very different and we
have scary thoughts.

Or we think we see scary things,
or hear strange sounds.

Does this happen to you?

It can be very good to have your favourite teddy
with you to cuddle in bed.

Some people like to go to sleep with the light on.

Do you?

Is there anything you need to help you feel good
about going to sleep?

Friends, Family, and School

It can be hard to talk about our problems and our fears or worries.

We can think that if we tell these things to other people who are sad too, we will make **their** worries worse.

So sometimes we keep our own troubles all shut up inside.

Can the person reading this with you help you with this?

It can be very difficult to keep all our troubles to ourselves.

Then we can feel like a jigsaw that is all muddled up.

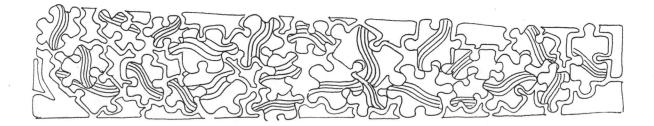

You might be worrying about who is going
to look after you now that your Special
Person has died.

Other grown-ups, or friends, or family,
will help.

Perhaps the person reading these pages with
you could talk to someone about your worries?

Would this be a good idea?

If so, who would you like them to talk to?

You might be worrying about
the other people who are sad with you.

You might be worrying that they
will be too sad to manage, or too tired,
perhaps, to look after you.

Do you have any
worries like these?

Perhaps you are afraid that
because one person has died,
someone else will die too.

Lots of people worry about
this if someone has died.
You can get so you are
worrying about so many
things, and so many people.

Is it like that for you?

When people are very sad,
they often get tired,
and sometimes they
cry a lot.

This doesn't mean that
they are going to die
as well.

When people are very sad, they can get very cross (angry).

Sometimes we feel very angry too.

This anger is because someone special has died.

The anger spills out all over other people in
our family, and sometimes over our friends
too.

So people are often very bad tempered
and unreasonable when they are sad.
This is hard to cope with, but it can help
to understand why this happens.
And it can help to talk about this too.

When people who are very sad get cross with us,
we can think everything is our fault.

Then we can get very worried that we are always
doing things wrong and making things worse.

Has this happened to you?

If it has, you are not the only person
this has happened to.

And sometimes the person who died might
have got cross too.

People do get cross when difficult things are happening to them.

135

When someone in the family dies it sometimes means
that other people have to do lots more jobs.

Has this happened in your family?

Do **you** have to do lots more jobs now?

Is this OK or is it hard for you?

Do you talk to one another in your family
about the person who has died?

At first it may seem very hard to do this,
but it is a good idea.

You can never forget the Special Person who died,
and so it is usually best to try to talk about them.

But this can be very hard to do, can't it?

Do your friends talk to you about the person who died?

Are things OK between you and your friends?

Often our friends find it very hard to know what to say to us…or even what to do.

Some people worry that their friends and other people at school or college might be talking about them behind their back.

This can be a hard problem.

Sometimes it can be useful for someone to talk to your teacher about this problem. Perhaps your mum or dad or someone else could help with this worry. Maybe the person reading this with you could help in some way?

Your teacher at school will be very sad that someone special to you has died.

Teachers want to help the children and young people in their school.

They will want to help you.

Many teachers are very pleased if we talk to them about how we would most like to be helped.

Then they can tell the others in your class what seems right for you.

And they may have ideas of their own that will be helpful for you while you are at school.

Maybe you can think of some ways your teacher could help you?

Lots of people find it extremely hard to think straight when something terrible has happened.

When we are sad we can sometimes go around as though we are in a thick fog, or cloud.

Then it is hard to think of anything at all.

Or our minds keep thinking of what has happened, or how sad we are. Thoughts keep coming into our minds to stop us thinking straight.

This is hard if you have lots of homework to do, or if you have to work hard in class. We can get into trouble for daydreaming, or not concentrating.

Has this happened to you?

If you have this problem it's a good idea to find someone to help you discuss this at school as soon as possible.

It is very lonely being sad at school.

And often it feels like you are the only person who has had such a terrible thing happen to them.

But there may be other sad children in your class who are feeling lonely too. Loneliness happens when we all go around keeping our sadness quietly inside us.

Can you think of anyone else you know who might be sad because of something that has happened to them?

You may not be the only person in your class feeling terrible.

It may help to talk to your teacher about how lonely, and how different, you feel at the moment.

Could someone help you to do this?

The playground can be
a very happy, busy place.

Or the playground can be
a very lonely place.

Which is it for you?

Do you like
your break-times at school?

What do you do at break
or in the lunch hour?

Are there particular people you like
to spend time with at school?

What a lot of questions for one page!

Just like being at school!!!!

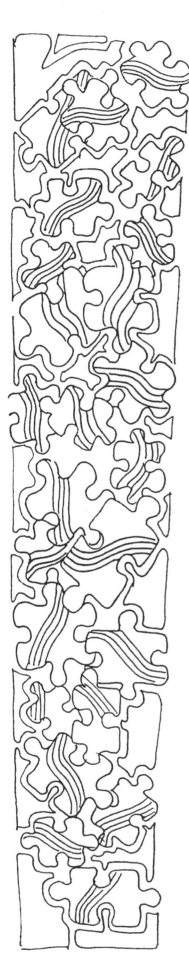

Sometimes at school we can find ourselves getting into trouble because we feel we want to do stupid things. Perhaps this has happened to you.

Sometimes children and young people get dared by others to do foolish or dangerous things. We might think that doing lots of wild things will help us forget our worries.

DON'T!!!

Doing dares and acting daft or wild may help people forget their worries, but it gets them into trouble, and makes a whole lot more worries.

If this is happening to you, can you talk about it?
It is important that you do.
Teachers are usually very helpful when they understand why people have got into a mess.

If these things are talked about they can be sorted out.

Things that are OK about school

Draw or write them here.

Things about school that I worry about

Draw or write them here.

Remembering

When a person dies, they leave us with
memories of things they did
or said, or how they were.

And so the person who has died lives
on in our memories.

The memories can be very happy ones.
Sometimes there are sad memories too.

We may want to talk about our memories,
or we may want to keep them to ourselves
for a while.

It is OK to remember.

It is also OK not to talk about memories
right now if you don't want to.

Some people want to talk more about
the Special Person who has died straight away.

Some people need to wait a while before they begin
to want to talk about their memories.

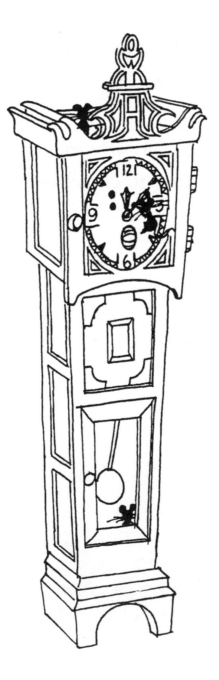

Sometimes we
remember things about
the person who has died that

make us sad

or angry

or worried.

Perhaps this person was
not always very nice.

Or perhaps you have some
other bad memory?

There can be good
memories, and
there can be bad memories.

Some people worry that they can't
remember what the person
who has died

looked like

or sounded like

or smelled like.

It can be dreadful to forget these
things.

It happens to lots of people
who are very sad.
But usually, after some weeks or so,
people remember these things again.

If you are worrying that you cannot
remember what your Special Person
was like, it may help you if you talk
about this difficulty.
But don't go trying to force yourself
to remember things. It is best to trust
that memories will come back
when they are ready!

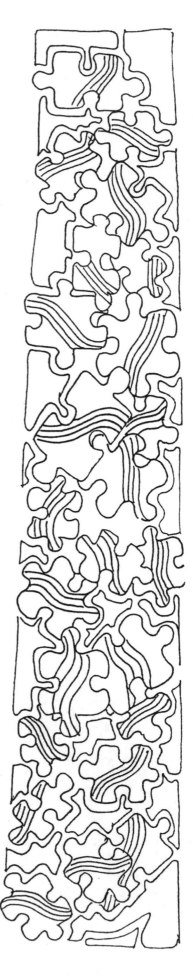

If someone was very special to us,
it makes sense that we need to
remember them, because they were
part of us, and we were part of them.

Remembering someone who has
died is often very painful.

But it can be a lovely thing to do.

If we talk about the person
it can also help us to feel a little better.

That sounds strange, but it's true.

There are lots of ways to help us remember
someone who has died.
We may want to think about this at once, or
we may want to wait.
Here are some ideas, and you may be able to
think of some of your own.

- Make a memory box: collect special
  things together that remind you of the person.

- Make a memory book with:

    photos

    letters

    poems

    pictures, etc.

- Make a tape of the person's favourite music.

- Talk to people with other memories to add to yours, or ask
  them to find photos, letters, or other things to add to your
  memory book. Or you could record them reminiscing
  (talking about their memories).

What else could you do?
What does 'remembering' mean to you?

Going On

Remember the leaves?

Winter can seem very long…
and very dark.

Sadness can seem very long and dark too.
But light does come back.

Happiness comes back too. Maybe not exactly the
same happiness can return; but you will know
happiness again.
In the winter the seeds are resting quietly in the
earth, waiting to grow in the spring.

Winter is a time when nature rests…
and watches…and waits.
Winter is a time for being cosy.

And so, too, in your sadness there will
be people to keep you safe and warm.
Spring will come.

Your Special Person will live in your
memories, and help to make you the
precious person you are.

Sadness will get easier.
Sunshine will come back.

My picture of life

Draw it here.

Spring

Everywhere there is death, there is new life.
Every spring the world changes colours
from dark to light.
New things grow from the earth;
Birds begin to sing, and make their nests.
We put away our winter woollens
and our Wellington boots.
There are kittens and lambs;
bees and butterflies.
New grass appears.
The sun grows stronger,
while the days get longer before
night time comes.

Spring brings life,
and light,
and warmth…and
hope that, somehow, we will go on.

We will go on hoping,
and growing,
and living,
and finding new
meaning and new
happiness.

For you

In the darkness there is a star, or a light,
or a candle, or the moon.

In the shadow the sun is never far away.

In the dark earth are the seeds of spring.

In our fears and worries lies also
our strength to overcome them.

In our sadness and tears there can also be
smiles and laughter.

In our being lonely and lost, there can be hope,
and people to comfort us.

Go well…

The end